GW00371655

# DUBLIN
# WIT

# DUBLIN WIT

## DES MacHALE

MERCIER PRESS
IRISH PUBLISHER – IRISH STORY

MERCIER PRESS

Cork

www.mercierpress.ie

© Des MacHale, 2011

ISBN: 978 1 85635 713 5

10 9 8 7 6 5 4 3 2 1

A CIP record for this title is available from the British Library

Printed and bound in the EU.

# CONTENTS

Introduction                                    9

The Floozie in the Jacuzzi                     11

Two Auld Wans on a Bus                         14

Brendan Behan and Family                       20

A Few Dublin Jokes                             30

Dean Jonathan Swift                            39

Dublin Football Jokes                          41

Culchie Jokes                                  47

Dublin Graffiti                                53

Northsider Jokes                               57

Dublin Wits                                    59

   Oscar Wilde                  59

   George Bernard Shaw          62

   Samuel Beckett               65

   Dave Allen                   65

   James Joyce                  66

   Seán O'Casey                 67

   Hugh Leonard                 68

   Oliver St John Gogarty       69

John D. Sheridan 69

Anthony Butler 70

Richard Brinsley Sheridan 71

John P. Mahaffy 72

Dublin's Mrs Malaprop 73

Moore Street 77

Misleading Advice for Tourists 83

A Final Flourish of Dublin Jokes 86

\*

*Dedication*
This book is dedicated, with much love,
to my sister-in-law Patricia, a true Dub.

\*

# INTRODUCTION

It is quite amazing that in a small island like Ireland we have so many different and distinctive kinds of wit and humour. The humour of Belfast is in a league of its own and in Galway and the West they regard themselves as the real custodians of Irish wit. The humour of Cork and Kerry is legendary while Waterford, Limerick and Wexford too have their own brand of hilarity. Even Sligo and Donegal can raise a chuckle if pressed.

But the wit and humour of our capital city, Dublin, reigns supreme, at least according to many Dubliners. Dublin wit has a cutting edge — the typical Dubliner not only believes he is superior, he *knows* he is superior. He has a healthy contempt for culchies, sheep stealers, yella bellies, cute Cork hoors, Orangemen, Kerrymen and other exotic rural varieties. Dublin humour can be cruel and unkind, sarcastic and hurtful, but it is clever, inventive and undoubtedly unique. The Dublin wit is not a happy bunny and lines are delivered without a smile, but the wit and humour of Dublin give a flavour to Irish humour that is famous worldwide. What other city in the world can boast a list of wits to compare with Wilde, Shaw, Swift, Behan, Sheridan (R.B. and J.D.), Joyce, Beckett, Allen, O'Casey, Leonard, Gogarty, O'Dea, Potter, Mahaffy and Butler?

This book is a tribute to the wit of Dublin and, dare I say it, the finest such collection of Dublin wit ever assembled. If you enjoy it, tell others. If not, in the words of Mo Po, save your breath for cooling your porridge!

*Des MacHale,* 2011

# THE FLOOZIE IN
# THE JACUZZI

In the boom times, the Irish firm of Smurfit donated the equivalent of a cool quarter of a million euro for an artistic statue of *Anna Livia*, a personification of the River Liffey, to be located in Dublin. It was a real work of art, but then anonymous Dublin wits got to work on her. First, she was covered in washing-up liquid and given a bubble bath. Then she was dubbed:

*The Floozie in the Jacuzzi*

Next she was called:

*The Hoor in the Sewer*

And then:

*The Mot on the Pot*

\*

This started a trend. The statue of poor old Molly Malone quickly became known as:

*The Tart with the Cart*

And then:

*The Dish with the Fish*

And finally:

*Bidet Mulligan*

\*

The statue of James Joyce with his cane was called:

*The Prick with the Stick*

\*

Oscar Wilde was dubbed:

*The Quare in the Square*

Or:

*The Fag on the Crag*

*

The sculpture of two auld wans sitting on a bench with their shopping near the Halfpenny Bridge became:

*The Hags with the Bags.*

*

The ill-fated algae-covered clock counting down the minutes to the millennium in the Liffey at O'Connell Bridge was known as:

*The Time in the Slime*

*The Scud in the Mud*

Or

*The Clock in the Dock*

*

The Spire in O'Connell Street that replaced the Floozie took a terrible hammering with names such as:

*Nelson's Revenge*

*The North Pole*

*The Nail in the Pale*

*The Stiletto in the Ghetto*

*The Rod to God*

*The Jab in the Slab*

*The Pin in the Bin*

*The Erection at the Intersection*

*The Taper near the Scraper*

*The Lampland in Clampland*

*The Spike in the Dyke*

And even:

*The Stiffy by the Liffey*

*

The statue of Patrick Kavanagh by the Grand Canal became *The Crank on the Bank*.

*

**Dublin rhyming slang is part of the language of the capital:**

A concert in the Phoenix Park is called *The Lark in the Park*.

*

The holy and sacred Bon Secours hospital is known as *The Bunch of Hoors*, or sometimes *The Bone Sick Cure*.

*

**And even when it does not rhyme, the witty corruption of Dublin place names is a capital art form:**

Glasnevin Cemetery has been called *The Dead Centre of Dublin* or even *Croak Park*.

*

Dublin's most famous Catholic church, because of its proximity to another region, has been called *The Pros' Cathedral*.

# TWO AULD WANS ON A BUS

**Two of the great stock characters of Dublin wit and humour are a pair of 'auld wans' – usually women but sometimes men – upstairs on a double-decker bus. A little learning, it has been said, is a dangerous thing, but in those hands, it can be absolute dynamite. Here are a few of their conversations that have been heard by the other passengers over the years, and honestly, even if you tried, you could not make them up.**

Two auld wans were passing a crematorium in a bus. Says one to the other, 'That's where they set the match to my mother. She wanted to be buried in a cemetery, and she doesn't know to this day that they cremated her.'

\*

'How's your son gettin' on in the army?' one auld wan on a bus asks another.

'He's getting on only terrific,' the other auld wan replies. 'He's in the army just six months and already they've made him a court marshal.'

\*

'Me kids have given me two tickets for Pavarotti as a birthday present,' says one auld wan to another.

'That's great,' says the other, 'is it for one week or two?'

\*

'I have one of the best sons a mother ever reared,' said the first auld wan.

'I agree wit yez,' says the second, 'sure he's always helpin' the police with their enquiries.'

*

'I had a meal in McDonalds for the first time last week,' said one auld wan to another on a bus.

'What did you think of it?' her companion asked.

'Well, I'll tell you one thing, he's come a long way since he had that farm.'

*

*First auld wan:* 'Me son Frank is paintin' the house for me this weekend.'

*Second auld wan:* 'But I thought he was in Mountjoy serving ten years for aggravated assault and battery.'

*First auld wan:* 'He's after gettin' time off for good behaviour.'

*Second auld wan:* 'It must be a great consolation for you to have such a good lad.'

*

The two auld wans were on a bus passing by the quays at low tide.

*First auld wan:* 'The river is very low at the moment isn't it?'

*Second auld wan:* 'I believe the breweries drain it every evening to make the porter.'

*

This time it's two auld fellas upstairs on a bus.

*First auld fella:* 'I was readin' in the paper the other day about all dem icebergs meltin' and floodin' de planet.'

*Second auld fella:* 'It's the greenfly effect.'

*

It's the two auld wans on the bus again.

*First auld wan:* 'I see where Biddy Mulligan has just cremated her fifth husband.'

*Second auld wan:* 'It's not fair — some of us can't get a man at all and other women have husbands to burn.'

*

The two auld wans were discussing body care and maintenance on the bus. 'I'm thinkin' of shavin' me legs,' says the first.

'They say it's a great way of losin' weight,' says the second.

*

'What do you think of the drugs problem in Dublin?' the first auld wan asks her friend.

'It's terrible,' says the second, 'but if it wasn't for the Valium, I'd be on the drugs meself.'

*

'Me sister is havin' a lung transplant,' says the first auld wan.

'Oh I don't know if I'd like that,' says the second, 'Swallowin' someone else's phlegm.'

*

It's the two auld fellas on the bus again.

*First auld fella:* 'Me daughter has taken up the opera and she's playin' the caterpillar in *Madame Butterfly*.'

*Second auld fella:* 'Maybe someday she'll be playin' the biscuit in the Marriage of Fig Roll.'

*

*First auld wan:* 'I don't know what to feed my cat.'

*Second auld wan:* 'Why don't you try him on Kit-E-Kat?'

*First auld wan:* 'He doesn't like chocolate.'

\*

'I'm goin' to night classes and learnin' Chinese,' says one auld wan to another on a bus.

'Why is that luv?' replies the other.

'Well me daughter and son-in-law have just adopted a Chinese baby and I want to be able to understand him when he begins to talk.'

\*

'I see Florrie went on holiday to Spain and died within twenty-four hours of arriving,' said one auld wan to the other.

'Dear oh dear,' said the other, 'there's nothing worse than dying on your holidays, and on top of that you feel so stiff the next day.'

\*

'I love the DART and the LUAS,' said one auld wan to the other.

'I think they're terrific too,' said the other auld wan, 'but they'll be even better when they circumcise the whole city.'

\*

'Wasn't it terrible about Jimmy Byrne?' said one auld wan to another.

'Why, what happened to him?' said the second auld wan.

'Well, he was working on a building site when a big

17

steam hammer dropped a hundred feet onto his chest and killed him stone dead.'

'I'm not surprised,' said the second auld wan, 'all the Byrnes had fierce weak chests.'

*

'I don't know what to get my son for his birthday,' said the first auld wan.

'Why not get him a book?' suggested the second auld wan helpfully.

'Don't be crazy,' said the first auld wan. 'He has a book already.'

*

'How's yer husband getting on in hospital?' one auld wan asks another.

'Not so good,' said the second, 'they've given him a post mortem operation.'

'What a pity they didn't give it to him sooner and they might have saved his life.'

*

The two auld wans on the bus were discussing the weather.

'Terrible changeable, isn't it,' said one, 'boiling one moment and freezing the next.'

'True for ye,' said the other, 'you wouldn't know what to pawn.'

*

Two auld wans went to a symphony concert at the National Concert Hall. The bus was a bit late so when they arrived it was after the interval.

'Now,' the conductor announced, 'we will have Beethoven's Fifth Symphony.'

'That's great,' smiled one auld wan to the other, 'we've missed four of them.'

*

'Me husband died,' said one auld wan to another in a bus, 'in an accident at Guinness' Brewery. He fell into a vat of porter and drowned.'

'Was it a sudden and painful death?' asked the other auld wan.

'No,' she replied, 'He got out three times to go to the gents.'

*

Believe it or not, thanks to new technology, one of the auld wans became pregnant and had a lovely baby.

Naturally, the other auld wan got on the bus to visit her and congratulate her. When she arrived, she handed over her present and said, 'Give us a look at the babbie, I'm dyin' to see it.'

'In a minute,' said the other auld wan, 'we'll have a cup of tea first.'

So they had a cup of tea and the second auld wan said, 'Can I see him now?'

'Hold on,' said the first auld wan, 'have a look at all his presents first.'

So they looked at all the presents, and the second auld wan said impatiently, 'When am I going to see him?'

'When he cries,' said the first auld wan, 'because I've forgotten where I've put him.'

# BRENDAN BEHAN AND FAMILY

Brendan Behan was the quintessential working-class Dublin wit, with a razor-sharp tongue and quicker on the draw with a humorous retort than anyone in Ireland or abroad. His quips and quotes are legendary and have filled whole books. Many hilarious stories and anecdotes surround him too and since his tragic death from the drink in 1964 these have multiplied and lost nothing in the telling. Here are some of the very funny quotes and sayings attributed to the 'bould' Brendan – he can lay claim to being one of the greatest Irish wits of all time and certainly as good as any that Dublin has produced.

The drink in that pub is not fit for washing hearses.

*

When I came back to Dublin I was court-martialled in my absence and sentenced to death in my absence, so I told them they could shoot me in my absence.

*

Shakespeare said pretty well everything and what he left out, James Joyce, with a nudge from meself, put in.

*

There is no bad publicity, except an obituary notice.

*

Kilbarrack, over by Howth, my father always maintained, was the healthiest graveyard in the country, with the sea air.

*

People never actually swim in Dublin Bay — they are merely going through the motions.

*

The first item on the agenda of every Irish organisation is 'The Split'.

*

The bars in Dublin are shut from 2:30 to 3:30 every afternoon. We call it the Holy Hour. The politician who introduced it was shot an hour afterwards.

*

America is the land of permanent waves and impermanent wives.

*

If it was raining soup, the Irish would be out with forks.

*

How about the raffle where the first prize was a week in Belfast and the second prize was two weeks in Belfast?

*

I'm a communist by day and a Catholic after it gets dark.

*

A job is death without the dignity.

*

I saw the ornithology correspondent of *The Irish Times*, a very prim and proper lady, one cold winter's afternoon across the street, so I shouted to her, 'How's the blue tits today missus?'

*

Critics are like eunuchs in a harem. They know exactly how it should be done, they see it done every night, but they cannot do it themselves.

*

A drama critic is like a bicycle without a saddle. They both give me a pain in the arse.

*

The impact of my play was like the banging together of two damp dishcloths.

*

God created alcohol just to stop the Irish from ruling the world.

*

I have never seen a situation yet so bad that a policeman couldn't make it worse.

*

When I'm healthy I'm not at all religious, but when I'm sick I'm very religious.

*

I'm a drinker with a writing problem.

*

Holy Father, there isn't a man in Dublin that wouldn't go to hell for you.

*

I first learned the use of whiskey at the age of six from my grandmother who said, 'Give him a sup of it now, and he will never know the taste of it when he grows up,' which I suppose is the biggest understatement of all time.

*

I'm staying alive only to save the funeral expenses.

\*

Cork people would steal the cross from behind Jesus' back and leave him hanging in mid-air.

\*

A message in my plays? What the hell do you think I am? A bloody postman?

\*

I'm not a politician — I have only one face.

\*

Yes we do have a bath in the house — but thank God we've never had to use it.

\*

Port wine will be supplied to those who are teetotallers in accordance with the well-known English custom.

\*

There was a fellow in prison whose lawyer was later known to boast that he had got his client a suspended sentence. They hanged him.

\*

I drink like a fish. The only difference is we drink different stuff.

\*

The only sort of man most women want to marry is a fella with a will of his own — made out in her favour.

\*

If there were only three Irishmen left in the world, you'd find two of them in a corner talking about the other.

\*

That fellow would drink porter out of a policeman's boots.

*

In prison we sometimes get food with our meals.

*

My family's land was all in window boxes.

*

I have forty acres of land in West Clare. When the tide is out.

*

All marriages are mixed — they're between men and women.

*

Anglo-Irishmen are people who ride horses, drink whiskey and read double-meaning books in Irish at Trinity College.

*

The number of people who buy books in Ireland would not keep me in drink for the duration of Sunday opening time.

*

I always carried gelignite; dynamite isn't safe.

*

The best words any man can hear at his funeral are: 'Carry on with the coffin. The corpse'll walk.'

*

When I was a kid I wanted to be a policeman but they found out my parents were married.

*

The posh lads in Dublin took piano lessons and dancing lessons but we took anything we could get our hands on that wasn't nailed down.

*

Even on his deathbed, Brendan Behan's wit did not desert him. To the nun who was looking after him, he smiled and said, 'Thank you sister; may you be the mother of an archbishop.'

*

**But it wasn't off the shelf that Brendan Behan took his wit and humour. His father, Da Stephen, had many a funny turn of phrase too:**

To a man who accidentally spilled a pint of stout over his trousers he said: May the Lamb of God stick his hind leg out through the golden canopy of heaven and kick the bollocks off you.

*

If you have money, spend it. First on necessities such as drink, and then if you have any left over, on luxuries such as food, clothes and shelter.

*

If Jesus had come down from the cross and married my wife, he'd be back up there in five minutes hammering the nails into himself.

*

When Stephen Behan was asked why he hadn't produced any plays himself, he replied: 'I was too busy producing playwrights.'

*

**And Brendan's mother Kathleen, the 'mother of all the Behans' was also a noted wit in her own right:**

I wouldn't trust my husband with a young woman for five minutes, and he's been dead for twenty-five years.

*

**Brendan's brother Dominic was a cynical wit too. He recounts a story of a rural Irish village:**

One day they opened a Catholic chapel, which was followed by a pub, a block of shops and eventually a school. The school went up last because there was no profit in it.

*

**And Brendan's other brother Brian could string a few funny words together too. As he said:**

Brendan lit a bonfire under the arse of Irish literature.

*

**Stories about Brendan Behan and his family are legion. It is of course, well nigh impossible to figure out which of these stories are true, but the following have a ring of authenticity about them:**

Brendan was being taken to Liverpool to serve a jail term but he got so drunk that they refused to let him into the prison! On another occasion he was barred from a pub he had never been in in his life. Talk about your reputation preceding you!

*

Brendan was once asked to explain the difference between poetry and prose at a literary gathering. He apparently did so by way of example, offering the following limerick:

There was a young fellow named Rollocks,
In employment with Ferrier Pollocks
As he walked on the strand,
With his girl hand in hand,
The water came up to his knees.

'Now,' explained Brendan, 'that was prose, but if the tide had been in, it would have been poetry.'

\*

Brendan once saw a sign in the window of a pub which said *All You Can Drink for £5*, so he went in and said to the barman, 'I'll have £10 worth of that.'

\*

Brendan once got a job in London working with a street repair gang. One morning he arrived at work to find all his fellow workers down in a huge hole in the road singing 'Happy Birthday to you'.

'Whose birthday is it?' he enquired.

'It's the hole's,' he was told, 'it's three years old today.'

\*

When Kathleen Behan was very ill her family informed her that she would have to go to a hospice for the dying.

'Horse piss?' she said to them. 'That's no drink for a dying woman.'

\*

Brendan once collapsed in a Dublin street and was rushed to hospital. Worried about his condition, the doctor decided to take a cardiograph and as the printout came up he said to his patient, 'Mr Behan, this is one of the most important things you have ever written.'

'And it's straight from me heart too, doctor,' quipped Brendan.

*

'Why do you drink so much alcohol?' a doctor once asked Brendan.

'What do you suggest I do with it, doc?' smiled Behan.

*

A penniless Brendan was once sitting in a bar with an empty glass in front of him. A friend took pity on him and said, 'Can I buy you another one, Brendan?'

As usual, Brendan was not stuck for a witty reply. 'Now what would I be doin' with another empty glass?' he countered with impeccable logic.

*

Brendan was wont to refer to the *fáinne*, the round pin worn by enthusiastic speakers of the Irish language, as *The Erse Hole*.

*

Not surprisingly, Brendan had many fans and even hangers-on. Once in a pub a fellow shouted to him, 'Do you remember when we were in the same brigade of the IRA?'

'Go away, ya bowsie,' retorted Brendan. 'The only brigade you ever saw active service in was the fire brigade!'

*

Brendan's description of an acquaintance:

A shrivelled-up seldom-fed bastard that had stolen money from under his dead mother's body and then put his hand on her breast and sworn he hadn't.

*

When Brendan visited Spain he was asked by a journalist if there was any bull-fighting in Ireland.

'Quite a lot,' he replied, 'but not between a bull and a matador. It's more likely to be two bulls fighting vigorously for the affections of a cow.'

*

Brendan once gave a pound to a beggarman who was expecting a bit more than that, so he hurled back abuse in return.

'I remember the time when you hadn't a penny to your name,' he taunted Brendan.

'You don't remember it half as well as I do, me oul' flower,' smiled Brendan.

*

Brendan was once asked by a reporter if he was an artist.

He replied, 'I am a true artist, a painter — a house painter that is. I am proud to share that profession with Adolf Hitler.'

# A FEW
# DUBLIN JOKES

The Dublin joke has a cutting edge – it is sarky, quite cruel, and very different from the type of joke you find in the rest of Ireland. The Dubliner is superior to his fellow countrymen and indeed to foreigners also, and the jokes reflect that fact. The Dublin woman too is no shrinking violet – she is verbally aggressive and inventive, loud and bawdy, and might have walked straight out of one of Seán O'Casey's plays. And though I hate to admit it, Dublin can lay claim to being the wittiest city in the world.

A Dublin mother was shouting at her young one running along the top of a high wall. 'Look,' she said, 'if you fall and break your legs, don't come runnin' to me.'

\*

Dubliners are a generous people and don't like meanness. In fact, some of their most scathing wit is directed towards tightwads. Here are a few examples:

That fella is so mean he wouldn't give you a slide if he owned the Alps.

\*

He's so mean he wouldn't tell you the time even if he had two watches.

*

He wouldn't give ya the steam off his piss.

*

I'm not sayin' he's mean but he's one of the few people I know that can peel an orange in his pocket.

*

He wouldn't give you a drink if he owned the Liffey.

*

He wouldn't give you a light if his arse was on fire.

*

That fella would skin a flea for the hide.

*

He tells the kids the ice cream vans play music only when they've run out of ice cream.

*

If you're playing poker in Dublin, it is useful to know what a Finglas flush is. That's any five cards and a gun.

*

That fella has no kids. He can't bring himself to part with anything.

*

For her birthday, his wife asked him for something with lots of diamonds in it so he bought her a pack of playing cards. Next year she told him she would like something long and flowing, so he threw her in the Liffey.

*

The work of Dublin Corporation outdoor employees has often been poetically described as 'breastfeeding their shovels.'

One morning a contingent of workmen arrived at the site and found that their shovels had not arrived. The foreman immediately phoned the headquarters for instructions.

He was told: 'Tell the men to lean against each other until the shovels arrive.'

*

What is orange and sleeps six?

A Dublin City Council repair truck.

*

This fellow called into the offices of Dublin Corporation and said to the man behind the desk:

'About the roof on our flat.'

'Yes,' said the official.

'We'd like one,' said the fellow.

*

Two Dublin girls were talking about their summer holidays.

'I spent a week in Majorca,' said one.

'Where's that?' asked the other.

'Dunno, we flew.'

*

This Dubliner went into a pub, ordered a pint, and was served with the worst drink he had ever tasted. When he complained to the publican he was told, 'You have only one pint, but I've got nearly a hundred barrels of the stuff.'

*

Two auld wans in a bus escaped from an earlier chapter and one of them was telling the other how her husband died suddenly. 'He went out in the garden,' she told her mate, 'to cut a head of cabbage, and dropped dead on the spot.'

'And what did you do?' asked her companion.

'I opened a tin of peas.'

\*

Dubliners are noted for their circumlocution — a Dubliner will never give you a straightforward 'yes' as an answer to a question, feeling that the point must be emphasised. Instead, he will answer, especially to the question, 'Would you like a pint?':

Can a duck swim?

Is the Pope a Catholic?

Does a rocking horse have a wooden dick?

Does Dolly Parton sleep on her back?

\*

When Walter Guinness of the Dublin brewing family was elevated to a peerage, he took the title Lord Moyne. Dublin wits were quick to remark 'Moyne's a Guinness' in pubs all over town.

\*

A little Dublin boy in school was asked to use the word 'bewitches' in a sentence. He said, 'You go on ahead; I'll be wit' yez in a minute.'

\*

How many Dublin trade unionists does it take to change a light bulb? Twelve — you gotta problem with that?

\*

What do you call a dead Dubliner?

A jack in the box.

\*

It had to be a Dubliner that first came up with the word testiculating. That means waving your hands about and talking bollocks.

*

Description of a Dublin gurrier: He'd gouge the two eyes outta yer head and come back and piss in the holes.

*

Description of a Dublin slapper: She had more fingerprints on her bottom than the database at Scotland Yard.

*

A Dublin truck driver was down the country and drove his truck under a low bridge. It got stuck and try as he might he could not move it forwards or backwards. The delighted locals gathered to gloat and one of them asked, 'Are you stuck?'

'No,' said the Dub, 'I was delivering this bridge and forgot the address.'

*

A Dubliner remarked that while sitting down he always hated to see a pregnant woman standing on the bus. So he always closed his eyes.

*

When the great Chubby Brown visited Dublin he was heckled with the line, 'Why are you so fat?'

He immediately retorted, 'Every time I sleep with your mother, she gives me a biscuit.'

*

An American was being driven round Dublin by a taxi driver.

'Say driver,' he said, 'I notice you have streets named after all your great patriots – Parnell, O'Connell, Tone and Emmet, but none after the greatest Irishman of all — Éamon de Valera. How come?'

'Well sur,' said the cabbie, 'we had no street long enough or crooked enough.'

*

A man and a woman were standing at a bus stop conversing with each other in the Irish language.

A true Dub sidled up to them and having listened uncomprehendingly to them for a few moments exploded, 'Look, why don't you two **** off back to yer own country?'

*

What is the traditional Dublin sex position?

Woman on her back in bed, man in the pub.

*

This Dubliner wasn't having much luck with the girls so he decided to go to a marriage agency. 'Look,' said the man in the agency, 'I've got just the woman for you. She's young, beautiful, intelligent, rich and a fantastic housekeeper.'

'But is she good in bed?' asked the Dub.

'Well,' said the man, 'some say she is, others say she's not.'

*

This auld Dublin wan was in hospital so another auld Dublin wan was visiting her. 'How are they looking after you?' asked the visitor.

'Not bad,' said the patient, 'but they said I must have an operation, so they've shaved me down there.'

'Down there?' said the visitor, 'I don't believe ya. Gwan, give us a look.'

35

'No I couldn't do that.'

'I'll pull the curtains round the bed,' said the visitor, so she did and had a look.

'Well, what d'ya think?' asked the patient anxiously.

'I think it suits ya,' said the visitor.

*

A Dubliner's description of a local girl — she's that ugly even the tide wouldn't take her out.

*

A Dubliner was wondering if he should join the British navy or the Irish navy. He finally decided on the Irish navy because he could cycle home for his tea every evening.

*

Where is the world-renowned Dublin Consultancy Clinic for the Impotent located?

Stillorgan, of course.

*

When the moon rock was brought back to the earth, every university in the world was given a sample on which to experiment. By an oversight, University College Dublin was not sent a piece and when they applied, all the moon rock was gone.

'Look,' said one NASA scientist to another, 'those Mick scientists won't know the difference — we'll send them a sample of highly compressed cow dung,' and they did.

After a year there was a huge international scientific conference at which all of the scientists presented their results. The UCD team came at the very end and everyone was waiting eagerly to hear their report. There was a hush when the team leader stood up to speak.

'We now have incontrovertible evidence,' he said, 'that the cow jumped over the moon.'

*

It is exceedingly dangerous to heckle a Dublin comedian on stage. Here are some of the retorts that hecklers have received over the years:

    I don't come and tell you how to do your job when
        you're selling *Big Issues*.
    If I want to hear an arse hole, I'll fart.
    Save your breath for blowing up your girlfriend.

*

The Royal College of Surgeons in Dublin has always trained African students. On one occasion, a lecturer in the RCSI noticed that the class he was teaching consisted entirely of African students. About ten minutes into the lecture the door opened and a local student arrived late. The lecturer went over to him, shook him by the hand and said 'Dr Livingstone, I presume?'

*

This Dubliner had three testicles so he thought he might make a bit of money betting about this fact. So one night he and a mate went into a pub and after a few drinks he said to the barman, 'I bet you €50 that between us, me and my mate have five testicles.'

'You're on,' said the barman, and the three of them proceeded to the gents for a quick visual verification.

As they were about to drop their trousers the Dubliner's mate said to him, 'I hope you have four, because I've only got one.'

*

A fellow once wrote a letter to Dublin City Council asking why whenever a car is causing an obstruction, the best solution they can come up with is to clamp it so that it can't be moved.

*

A giraffe goes into a Dublin bar and asks the barman, 'Has my brother been in recently?'

'I don't know,' said the barman, 'what does he look like?'

*

A Dubliner goes into a bank and points a gun at the cashier and says, 'Hand over the money or you're Geography.'

'Surely you mean History,' says the cashier.

'Don't change the subject,' says the Dubliner.

*

A skeleton walks into a Dublin bar and the barman asks him what he'll have.

'I'll have a pint of Guinness,' says the skeleton, 'and a mop please.'

*

A Dubliner goes to the barber for a shave and complains he can never get a close shave on his cheeks.

'Here,' says the barber, 'put this wooden ball in your mouth and press it up against your cheek.'

The guy did so and got the closest shave imaginable on his cheek.

'What happens if I swallow it?' he asked anxiously.

'Just wait a couple of days and return it,' said the barber, 'like the other customers do.'

# DEAN JONATHAN SWIFT

Dean Jonathan Swift may or may not have been a real Dubliner, but it is probable that he was born in Dublin on 30 November 1667 of Yorkshire descent. When he was about a year old, he was kidnapped by his nurse and taken from Dublin to the north of England where he remained for three years. After a stormy career in religion and politics during which he wielded a vicious pen, he was banished to his native Dublin in 1713 and became Dean of St Patrick's Cathedral, where he was to remain for the rest of his life. Swift became one of the English language's greatest masters of irony and satire, but his wit had a vicious Dublin edge to it, which makes it timeless. He championed the Dublin poor who surrounded him on all sides and to revenge himself on his English tormentors, he supported several Irish causes. Here are some examples of his distinctive wit:

A tavern is a place where they sell madness by the bottle.

*

I never knew any man in my life who could not bear another's misfortune perfectly like a Christian.

*

If a lump of soot falls into the soup, and you cannot conveniently get it out, stir it well in and it will give the soup a French taste.

\*

I propose that a tax be levied on female beauty. Let every woman be permitted to assess her own charms — then she'll be generous enough.

\*

Never remark in England that the air in Ireland is healthy and excellent or they will most certainly tax it.

\*

If the church and the devil went to law, the devil would win, for all the lawyers and attorneys would be on his side.

\*

Under an oak in stormy weather;
I joined this rogue and whore together;
And none but he who rules the thunder
Can pull this rogue and whore asunder.

\*

All political parties die of swallowing their own lies.

\*

A very little wit is valued in a woman as we are pleased with a few words spoken plain by a parrot.

\*

When men grow virtuous in their old age, they only make a sacrifice to God of the devil's leavings.

# DUBLIN FOOTBALL JOKES

**The Dublin Gaelic football team – the Sky Blues – are among the most fanatically supported outfits in the whole world of sport. Hill Sixteen in Croke Park is their stronghold – a place no Kerryman or Corkman or Galwayman would be seen dead in, or alive for that matter. The wit of a Dublin football crowd is legendary, aimed at the opposition, the referee, or nobody in particular. But for all this support, since the 1970s the Dublin team has failed to deliver the goods on many occasions and bring Sam Maguire back to the capital. Dublin supporters are generally philosophical, but they have been known to turn their wit against their own beloved team:**

They say there are only two things visible on the earth when a man is standing on the moon — the Great Wall of China and the gaping hole in the Dublin defence.

*

What's the difference between O.J. Simpson and the Dublin football team?

O.J. had a better defence.

*

Dublin supporters have been known to direct their fire at their own side when things go wrong on the field.

Among remarks they have been known to make are the following:

That fellow is about as useful as tits on a bull.
That fellow is as useless as a chocolate teapot.
That goalkeeper is as useful as a trapdoor in a canoe.
The referee is about as useful as a one-legged man at an arse-kicking contest.

\*

One Dublin supporter asked another, after yet another heavy defeat by Kerry, 'Where did it all go wrong in Croke Park today?'

Replied his mate, 'On that big green bit in the middle.'

\*

A Dublin footballer is in a supermarket when he sees an old lady struggling with some heavy bags. 'Can you manage?' he asks her.

'No way,' she says, 'I wouldn't take on the Dublin team for any money.'

\*

Pessimists say the cup is half empty. Optimists say the cup is half full. Dubliners have never even seen the cup.

\*

The Dublin football trophy room has just been broken into and the entire contents stolen. The gardaí are looking for two men carrying a sky-blue carpet.

\*

This fellow from Mayo was up in Dublin for the big match but never having been in the capital before, he was seriously lost. He asked a Dubliner, 'How do I get to Croke Park?'

'Practice man, practice,' quipped the Dubliner.

*

A Dubliner and a Kerryman were discussing the fact that Dublin had not won an All-Ireland senior football title for so many years.

'What advice would you give us,' asked the Dub, 'seeing as you come from the Kingdom, the home of football?'

'Well,' said the Kerryman, 'my advice to you is to go down to Kerry, choose thirty nice young Kerry girls, bring them up to Dublin and within a generation their children will form a Dublin football team that will win an All-Ireland. But for God's sake, make sure they are pregnant before they leave Kerry.'

*

As an RTÉ commentator once remarked, 'If Lee Harvey Oswald had been a Dublin forward, John F. Kennedy would still be alive and kicking.'

*

A Dublin footballer was caught speeding in his car while driving up the motorway. He explained to the judge that it was the only way he could get a few extra points.

*

The Dublin trophy room — I've seen more silver on a Kit Kat.

*

What is the difference between a tennis player and a Dublin forward?

A tennis player sometimes puts the ball in the net.

*

A man was walking his greyhound on a Dublin beach when he stubbed his toe on an old lamp. He picked up the lamp and rubbed it clean and out popped a genie!

'Your wish is my command, Master,' said the genie. 'What can I do for you?'

'Well,' said the man, 'could you make my dog win the Greyhound Derby?'

'Take it easy,' said the genie, 'that greyhound must be twenty years old. I'm a bit out of practice lying in that lamp for the last thousand years, so could you set me a more realistic task please?'

'Well,' said the man, 'could you make Dublin win the All-Ireland senior football title next September?'

'Give me another look at that old dog,' said the genie.

*

Snow White arrived home to find her cottage on fire — the whole place was a blazing inferno.

'Oh no,' she cried, 'My friends, the seven dwarves, will all be killed.'

Then she heard a voice singing out 'Dublin for the Sam Maguire.'

'Thank goodness,' she said to herself, 'at least Dopey is still alive.'

*

The Dublin manager approached the subs dugout after a heavy defeat. 'As for you bunch of layabouts,' he said to them, 'you're not even good enough to play for this shower of useless losers.'

*

A Dublin lad was going on his holidays to Kerry so his father took him aside and gave him a bit of advice.

'Be careful with your money now, lad,' he told him, 'and always examine your change when you are in a pub or a shop. Those unscrupulous Kerry people will often try to pass you an All-Ireland medal instead of a two-euro coin.'

*

Three Irish football fans were allowed to ask God one question:

'When will Kildare next win the All-Ireland football title?' the Kildare fan asked God.

'Not for twenty years,' answered God and the Kildare fan went away crying.

'When will Mayo next win the All-Ireland football title?' the Mayo fan asked.

'Not for a hundred years,' answered God and the Mayo fan went away crying.

'When will Dublin next win the All-Ireland football title?' the Dublin fan asked God, and God went away crying.

*

What is the definition of a late tackle in a Dublin football match?

One that happens the day after the game.

*

First Dublin fan: 'I just got a sky-blue jersey for the wife.'

Second Dublin fan: 'Great swap!'

*

The Dublin backs formed a defensive wall for a close-in free but a Kerry forward drove the ball low and hard and hit one of them in a very painful spot indeed.

The injured player was rushed to the hospital screaming. 'Will I ever play for Dublin again?' he asked the doctor.

'Certainly,' smiled the doctor, 'but only for the ladies team.'

*

The Dublin County Football Board are in big trouble with the taxman. It seems they have been claiming for silver polish for the last twenty years.

*

If Dublin ever discover that Gaelic Football is a team game, then all the other counties are in big trouble.

*

And let us not forget Dublin hurling — described by one Corkman as 'some sort of compulsory tillage'.

# CULCHIE JOKES

There are several theories about the origin of the word 'culchie'. Some believe that it comes from Kiltimagh (Coillte Mach) in County Mayo, while others attribute it to Clonakilty (Cloch na gCoillte) in County Cork. However, when my good friend, Paddy Rock, a true Dubliner now resident in the lovely village of Clonbur in County Galway, was setting up his Culchie Festival, he delved deeply into the derivations of the word. It turns out that culchie comes from agricultural students in Dublin's UCD whose country ways came in for notice from the 1930s onwards. One thing is for sure – the culchie is still a figure of fun in Dublin.

Have you heard about the culchie who went to Egypt to become a pyramid salesman?

*

Why do culchies never play hide and seek?
Nobody ever wants to look for them.

*

This culchie went up to Dublin to make a fortune as a con artist. However, the first Dubliner he tried to sell the Millennium Spire to turned out to be the owner of the thing and the culchie had to pay him €500 to stop him reporting the incident to the police.

*

Why do Dubliners take an instant dislike to culchies?

It saves time.

*

A Dubliner bet a culchie that he could prove he was Jesus Christ.

'You're on,' said the culchie, 'I bet you €100 you're not.'

So they went into a bar and as soon as the barman saw the Dubliner he said, 'Jesus Christ, are you here again?'

*

This culchie went up to Dublin and got a job driving a one-man double-decker bus. One day the bus crashed and was a write-off and dozens of passengers were injured. At the official inquiry the culchie was asked how the accident happened.

'Don't blame me,' said the culchie, 'I was upstairs collecting fares at the time.'

*

Sex Manual for Culchies:

In, out. Repeat if necessary.

*

A culchie was describing how all his friends laughed at him when he said he was going to Dublin to become a comedian.

'Well I'll tell you one thing,' he said, 'they're not laughing now.'

*

Another culchie went to Dublin and got a job as a taxi driver. But he soon quit because he was fed up with people talking behind his back.

*

What is the difference between a culchie and a white line on the road?

You shouldn't run over a white line.

\*

A Dubliner claimed that culchies make better lovers — ask any cow, he smiled.

\*

Why are culchies buried with their arses sticking up out of the ground?

So that Dubliners can park their bicycles.

\*

A culchie went to Dublin and got a job as a postman. The pay wasn't much but it was as good as walking the streets on the dole.

\*

Why do culchies make such poor card players?

Every time they pick up a spade, they spit on their hands.

\*

A culchie broke into a gambling casino in Dublin. When the police caught him he was €5,000 down.

\*

Two culchies, one very thin and the other very fat, jump together from the top of Liberty Hall. Which one hits the ground first?

Who cares, so long as they are both culchies.

\*

Have you heard about the culchie who won a spot prize at a dance?

He had 5,329 spots.

\*

Two culchies were playing a game of snooker but didn't pot a single ball all night.

'Next time,' a friendly Dubliner advised them, 'take that wooden triangle from around the balls.'

*

A culchie asked a Dubliner why Dubliners were so smart.

'It's our diet,' said the Dub, 'and if you give me €100, I'll sell you some food that will make you smart too.'

'Done,' said the culchie, so the Dub sold him a pound of Moore Street fish heads and the culchie ate them.

When the culchie had bought his third batch of fish heads for €100, he said to the Dub, 'Hold on a minute – I can buy those fish heads for fifty cent in Moore Street.'

'Right,' said the Dub, 'just look how smart you're getting already.'

*

Why has Australia got all the kangaroos and Dublin got all the culchies?

Australia had first choice.

*

A culchie newly arrived in Dublin was asked what he thought of the Millennium Spire. 'It looks very nice,' he replied, 'but they'll never get it off the ground.'

*

Why do culchies have big noses?

Culchies have big fingers.

*

What did a culchie do when his wife had twins?

He went out with a shotgun looking for the other man.

*

Have you heard about the culchie who was stranded for an hour in a big department store when the escalator broke down?

*

A culchie arrived up in Dublin and stood looking up at Liberty Hall. A Dub arrived on the scene and said, 'Look, you've got to pay me €10 for every storey of Liberty Hall you look at. How many storeys did you look at?'

'Five,' said the culchie, and handed over €50.

'I certainly fooled him,' said the culchie to himself afterwards, 'I really looked at ten storeys.'

*

This rich bloke from the midlands pulled into a derelict car park on the Dublin quays and parked his Mercedes containing a savage Alsatian on the back seat. A little Dublin urchin crawled out of the rubble with his hand out and enquired, 'Mind yer car for ya, mister?'

'No thank you,' smiled the visitor to the capital, 'I think the dog will be sufficient protection for the vehicle.'

As the man departed, the urchin said, 'Can yer dog put out a fire mister?'

*

How do you recognise a culchie in a car wash?

He's the one sitting on his motorbike.

*

A culchie saw a sign on the window of a garda station:

MAN WANTED FOR ARMED ROBBERY

So he went in and applied for the job.

*

A culchie went into Dublin's GPO to buy a licence for his dog.

'Name please,' said the clerk.

'Rover,' said the culchie.

\*

A huge British ship was steaming into Dublin Bay. At the last moment, the captain realised his channel was not clear so he radioed, 'Give way — this is a ship of Her Majesty's fleet.'

'Sorry,' came the voice back, 'We cannot do that sir.'

'Look, you Irish idiot,' said the captain, 'give way or there will be a serious accident.'

'No,' came the reply, 'you give way.'

'For the last time,' said the captain, 'give way or I cannot be responsible for the consequences.'

'This is the Kish Lighthouse,' said a voice with a strong Dublin accent, 'your call.'

\*

This oriental tourist in Dublin was looking for the Botanic Gardens but he was seriously lost. 'Excuse please,' he said to a passing Dubliner, 'where is Botanic Gardens?'

'No problem,' said the Dub, 'I know that well. You go down to Finglas and turn left. No, that's not right. You go to Marino and turn right — no, that's not right either. The Botanic Gardens — sure I know them as well as the back of me own hand.'

'Where is Botanic Gardens?' said the gentleman impatiently.

'I have it,' said the Dub. 'Tell me, do you know Slattery's in Terenure?'

# DUBLIN GRAFFITI

*In a hospital loo*: The human body, properly looked after, will last a lifetime.

\*

*In a pub:* Avoid the Saint Paddy's Day Rush — get drunk now.

\*

*On a public notice board:* Keep Dublin tidy — dump your litter in Wicklow.

\*

*In the jacks of a pub:* Reality is an illusion created by a lack of alcohol.

\*

*In the Dáil jacks:* Leinster House is like a septic tank — all the really big chunks rise to the top.

\*

*In Trinity College:* The ideal wife for a Dubliner is a rich dumb blonde nymphomaniac who owns a pub near a golf course.

\*

*At Heuston Station:* Dial a Culchie — Ring 999.

\*

*Near O'Connell Bridge:* Cut out the middle man — Pee directly into the Liffey.

\*

*In a ladies' loo:* Never trust a man with testicles.

*In Dundrum Shopping Centre:* Sex is what people from Foxrock keep their potatoes in.

*

*In a pub toilet:* A true Dubliner would trample over the bodies of twelve naked women to reach a pint of porter.

*

*In a hotel loo:* Don't complain about the beer in the bar — you'll be old and weak yourself someday.

*

*Near Dáil Éireann:* If bullshit was music an Irish TD would be a brass band.

*

*Near Donnybrook:* RTÉ stands for really terrible entertainment.

*

*In Clontarf:* if Brian Boru hadn't gone to his tent to pray — the chances are he would still be alive today.

*

*In Donnybrook:* Show me a Dubliner who gives his seat to a lady on the bus and I'll show you a man who is getting off at the next stop.

*

*In a dockland pub:* Water is a fine drink if taken in the right spirit.

*

*In the gents at UCD:* Exams are the best cure for constipation.

*

*In Heuston Station:* Wanted — teabag driers for Iarnrod Éireann.

*Near Kildare Street:* The main difference between Dáil Éireann and a cactus is that a cactus has all its pricks on the outside.

*

*In a public toilet in Dalkey:* Incoming traffic has the right of way.

*

*In a Drumcondra pub:* Take crime off the streets and put it back in Leinster House where it belongs.

*

*In Middle Abbey Street:* A Dublin journalist is a man who stays sober until lunchtime.

*

*In a pub toilet:* Work is the curse of the drinking classes.

*

*In a psychiatric hospital:* Give generously to mental health week — or I'll kill you.

*

*In the Dáil chambers:* Leinster House is the original political asylum.

*

*In a golf club loo:* It was a quiet wedding — her father had a silencer on the shotgun.

*

*In a suburban hotel:* I had a brass band at my wedding, it was on my wife's finger.

*

*In the bog of a fee-paying Dublin school:* This is a refuge for emotionally disturbed teachers.

*

*In the toilets at DCU:* Girls are like toilets — vacant, engaged or full of crap.

*

*Near Saint Stephen's Green:* Free women — where? Where?

*

*In Leinster House:* Women TDs are just men who worked their balls off.

*

*In Belfield:* DCU is just UCD for dyslexics.

*

*On a wall near Dáil Éireann:* The difference between Robin Hood and the Government is that Robin Hood stole from the rich to give to the poor.

*

*In Heuston Station:* I used to drive a train for Irish Rail but I was sacked for overtaking.

*

*On O'Connell Bridge:* Keep Dublin tidy — stay in bed.

*

*On a bus shelter:* I have a soft spot for politicians — the Bog of Allen.

*

*On a telephone box:* A meeting of all Dublin virgins will take place in this phone box at 8 p.m. tonight.

# NORTHSIDER
# JOKES

Almost every modern city has a northside–southside divide and Dublin is no exception. For some reason or other, the northsiders seem to come off worse in the joke stakes. Here are a few examples:

What do you call a lamp-post on the northside?
    A leisure centre.

*

What do you call a northsider in a suit?
    The defendant.

*

What do you call a car containing two northsiders that isn't blaring loud music?
    A police car.

*

Why shouldn't you hit a northsider with your car when he's riding a bike?
    It might be your bike.

*

What do you call a northsider in a semi-detached house?
    A burglar.

*

Why do cars on the northside have such small steering wheels?

So you can drive them wearing handcuffs.

*

What does a dog on the northside say?

Jaysus woof.

*

What do you call a northsider in a Mercedes?

A joyrider!

*

An English teacher in a school in Dublin's northside was doing 'opposites' with her class. 'What is the opposite of day?' she asked.

'Night,' chanted the class.

'And what is the opposite of arrive?'

'Depart,' they chanted.

'And what is the opposite of buy?'

'Rob,' they all chanted.

*

How do we know Batman is a northsider?

He never goes out without Robin.

*

A southsider was visiting his grandmother on the northside. 'When I was a girl,' she told him, 'I could go out with a shilling and come home with a loaf of bread, a bottle of milk, a pound of sausages, a chicken, four lamb chops, twenty cigarettes and a dozen eggs. I can't do that nowadays.'

'It's terrible,' said the grandson, 'but that's inflation for you.'

'It's nothing to do with inflation,' said the granny. 'It's all those bloody CCTV cameras in the shops nowadays.'

# DUBLIN WITS

## OSCAR WILDE

Oscar Wilde, born in Dublin, was Ireland's greatest wit and perhaps even the greatest wit the human race has produced. In contrast with Behan, Wilde was sophisticated, erudite and urbane, but his Dublin origins gave a sharp edge to his wit, and audiences all over the world still roll in the aisles at his aphorisms, well over a hundred years after his death. There are whole books of Wilde's wit containing hundreds of examples so it would be repetitious to quote them here again, but no tribute to the wit of Dublin would be complete without some mention of the 'bould Oxter':

One should never listen. To listen is a sign of indifference to one's hearers.

*

The view from a hotel window is immaterial except to the hotelier, who of course charges it on the bill. A gentleman never looks out of the window.

*

I am a man of regular habits. I am always in bed by four or five.

*

In prison, I studied German. Indeed, this seems to be the proper place for such study.

*

We must present ourselves at Holloway Gaol at four o'clock. After that, it is difficult to gain admission.

*

It is always painful to part from people whom one has known for only a brief time. The absence of old friends one can endure with equanimity.

*

After a good dinner, one can forgive anybody, even one's own relations.

*

My dear delightful company, I have just watched your performance of *The Importance of Being Earnest*. It reminded me of a play I once wrote.

*

I like Wagner's music better than anybody's. It is so loud that one can talk the whole time without other people hearing what one says.

*

Niagara Falls are the bride's second greatest disappointment.

*

I do not have any religion — I am an Irish Protestant.

*

The only thoroughly original ideas I have ever heard Mr Whistler express have had reference to his superiority as a painter over painters greater than himself.

*

When I was young I used to think that money was the most important thing in life. Now that I am old, I know it is.

*

I never travel without my diary. One should always have something sensational to read on the train.

*

I worked on one of my poems all day. In the morning I put in a comma and in the afternoon I took it back out again.

*

The General was essentially a man of peace — except of course in his domestic affairs.

*

Poor old Lord Mortlake, who had only two topics of conversation: his gout and his wife. I never could quite make out which of the two he was talking about.

*

I have to choose between this world, the next world and Australia.

*

Know him? I know him so well that we haven't spoken to each other for over ten years.

*

I regret I must decline your invitation owing to an engagement I am just about to make.

*

It is very easy to endure the difficulties of one's enemies. It is the successes of one's friends that are hard to bear.

*

You should study the peerage; it is the best thing in fiction the English have done.

*

The English country gentleman galloping after a fox — the unspeakable in pursuit of the uneatable.

*

Football is all very well a good game for rough girls, but not for delicate boys.

*

It is very kind of the impressionist to tell us who he is mimicking. It saves discussion.

# GEORGE BERNARD SHAW

**Shaw was another world-class wit born in Dublin. While perhaps lacking the incisive and devastating accuracy of Wilde, Shaw was a superb social commentator whose quips, jibes and quotes are as relevant today as they were when he penned them. Again, Shaw's wit would fill a whole book, so in this anthology we will confine ourselves to the twenty or so that I believe are among his best. Shaw is a more benign figure than Wilde and his wit therefore has less impact.**

I am an unbeliever but I sometimes have doubts.

*

Certainly I enjoyed myself at your party. There was nothing else to enjoy.

*

I am informed that Lady Marlborough will be AT HOME on the 26th. So will I.

*

Which painting in the National Gallery would I save if there was a fire? The one nearest the door of course.

*

Only lawyers and mental defectives are automatically exempt from jury duty.

*

Two people getting together to write a book is like three people getting together to have a baby. One of them is superfluous.

*

Nature, not content with denying him the art of thinking, conferred on him the gift of writing.

*

An Englishman thinks he is being moral when he is only being uncomfortable.

*

Marriage will always be a popular institution because it combines a maximum of temptation with a maximum of opportunity.

*

He knows nothing and thinks he knows everything. That points clearly to a political career.

*

Nothing soothes me more after a long and maddening course of piano recitals than to sit and have my teeth drilled.

*

Women want other women's husbands like horse-thieves prefer a horse that is broken in to one that is wild.

*

She had lost the art of conversation, but not, unfortunately, the power of speech.

*

My father must have had some elementary education, for he could read and write and keep accounts inaccurately.

*

I came across a book I had signed 'With compliments' to a friend, in a second-hand bookshop. So I bought it and sent it to him signed 'With renewed compliments'.

*

In baseball I see no reason why the infield should not try to put the batter off his stride at the critical moment by neatly timed disparagement of his mother's respectability.

*

The French don't care what they do as long as they pro-nounce it properly.

*

The spectacle of twenty-two grown men with hairy legs chasing a bladder filled with air from one end of the field to another is both ludicrous and infantile.

*

Go on writing plays, my boy. One of these days a London producer will go into his office and say to his secretary, 'Is there a play from Shaw this morning?' and when she says 'No', he will say, 'Well, then we'll have to start on the rubbish.' And that's your chance, my boy.

*

He who can, does; he who cannot, teaches.

*

Am I Shaw? I'm positive.

# SAMUEL BECKETT

Beckett, known more widely as a serious writer, had a finely tuned sense of humour and some of his novels, approached from the correct angle, are downright hilarious. He is reputed to have submitted his MA thesis to his *alma mater*, Trinity College Dublin, written entirely on lavatory paper! Here are a couple of his wittier remarks:

Dublin University contains the cream of Ireland — rich and thick.

*

It has been said that my *Godot* is a play in which nothing happens — twice.

# DAVE ALLEN

David Tynan O'Mahony, better known as Dave Allen, was born in the Dublin suburb of Tallaght in 1936. He was related to one of Ireland's best-known poets, Katherine Tynan, and also Eoin O'Mahony, a mellow-tongued barrister, travelling scholar and one of Ireland's best storytellers, known to all as 'The Pope.'

**Dave Allen was one of the finest wits that Dublin has produced, but it was on British TV that he made his biggest mark.**

Ireland is the only place in the world where procrastination takes on a sense of urgency.

*

My bank manager went for a heart transplant but they couldn't find a stone of the right size.

*

My favourite retort to hecklers is, 'If I had a head like yours I'd have it circumcised.'

*

Ireland has one of the world's heaviest rainfalls. If you see an Irishman with a tan, it's rust.

*

My church accepts all denominations — fives, tens, twenties.

*

I'm an atheist, thank God.

# JAMES JOYCE

**There is some cynical humour in the works of the 'bould Jimmy Joist', but you have to search pretty hard. He once described a singer as having 'a base barreltone voice' and that's about as good as he gets. Other attempts at humour include:**

You may certainly not kiss the hand that wrote *Ulysses*.

It's done lots of other things as well.

*

Become a Protestant? Certainly not. Just because I've lost my faith doesn't mean I've lost my reason.

*

'When I makes tea,' as old mother Grogan said, 'I makes tea. And when I makes water I makes water.'

*

When he told his father he was about to marry Nora Barnacle, he replied, 'Now there's a girl that will stick to you.'

*

Nora Joyce is reputed to have said, 'James, why don't you write books that people can understand?' And, 'If only James had stuck to music, we might have made some money.'

## SEÁN O'CASEY

**Seán O'Casey was yet another Dublin wit, but his humorous quotes are a bit thin on the ground.**

I never heard him cursing; I don't believe he was ever drunk in his life — sure he's not like a Christian at all.

*

I'm telling you Joxer, the whole world's in a state of chassis.

# HUGH LEONARD

Hugh Leonard, whom I was privileged to number among my friends, was a Dubliner, well almost. Though he won fame as a dramatist, he was essentially a superb wit, scathing and irreverent with a devastating turn of phrase. Here are a few of his best bon mots:

Drama critics are there to show gay actors what it is like to have a wife.

*

My grandmother made dying her life's work.

*

The problem with Ireland is that it is a country full of genius, but absolutely no talent.

*

It was embarrassing. I felt like a figure skater who had forgotten to put on her knickers.

*

Never under any circumstances write comedy for laughs. This is as ruinous as believing your wife means it when she says, 'Tell me all about her. I swear I don't mind.'

*

All our operators are either drunk or fornicating right now, but if you care to leave a message when you hear the tone ...

*

Daddy, when I'm grown up I want to become an actor.
    Don't be greedy son, you can't be both.

*

If you are inserting a suppository last thing at night, always take your socks off first, and if you are inserting a suppository first thing in the morning always ensure that your socks are on first. Bending over can cause the things to fly out with great velocity and there is always the danger of ricochet. Once I broke a holy statue.

## OLIVER ST JOHN GOGARTY

**Gogarty was one of the most sophisticated of Dublin wits. His material is largely for honours students only!**

There is no such thing as a large whiskey.

\*

When Saint Patrick first visited Ireland, there was no word in the Irish language to express sobriety.

\*

William Orpen never got under the surface until he got under the sod.

## JOHN D. SHERIDAN

**Sheridan, John D., is one of our most under-rated wits. His humour is gentle and mocking and always hits its target in its unerring observation of Irish life, urban and rural.**

The first rule of hospitality is that the visitor must never get a glimpse of the conditions in which you normally live.

*

What prompted me to take up writing? Well, in the first place, the sandwich board used to chafe me.

*

This book is dedicated to whom it may concern.

*

Once a woman has decided to knit a jersey, nothing short of total paralysis will stop her.

*

'Stance' is defined by the Rules of Golf as 'that which you have taken up when you place your feet on the ground in position for and preparatory to striking the ball'. The location of the feet before they are placed on the ground is left to the discretion of the individual player.

*

When my wife is away and I am left to keep house for myself, I know it is time to do the washing-up when I put something on the kitchen table and something falls off the other end.

# ANTHONY BUTLER

**Tony Butler, whom I had the pleasure of meeting several times, was a down-to-earth bacon and cabbage wit, and a true Dubliner.**

The management of an Irish pub cannot be held responsible

for any accidents which occur in the mad rush for the doors at closing time.

*

The Irish climate is wonderful, but the weather ruins it.

*

In Ireland when the weather forecast is bad, it's invariably correct; when it's good, it's invariably wrong.

*

Many of our politicians have died for Ireland, and will do so again if necessary.

# RICHARD BRINSLEY SHERIDAN

**Sheridan, R.B., was the author of *The Rivals* and the man who gave us the name 'Malaprop'. He was one of the foremost wits of his day. This is a little sample of his output:**

I think the interpreter is the harder to understand of the two.

*

I handed one of my creditors an IOU and thought, thank God that's settled.

*

It is not in my interest to pay the principal nor in my principle to pay the interest.

*

The right honourable gentleman is indebted to his memory for his jests, and to his imagination for his facts.

A Limerick banker had an iron leg and it was the softest thing about him.

*

When my son Tom announced that he would proclaim his independence of party as an MP by writing the words *To Let* on his forehead, I advised him to write underneath *Unfurnished*.

# JOHN P. MAHAFFY

**Mahaffy was one of Dublin's greatest wits of the nineteenth century. His world centred on Trinity College Dublin and he rarely ventured outside its walls. Nevertheless, his wit is both cosmopolitan and legendary.**

What the difference between a man and a woman is I cannot conceive.

*

In Ireland the inevitable never happens but the impossible always does.

*

An Irish bull is always pregnant.

*

I am told that Traill is ill. Nothing trivial I hope.

*

No one ever sank to the depths of evil all at once: it takes forty years to become a Senior Fellow at Trinity College, Dublin.

# DUBLIN'S
# MRS MALAPROP

**The malapropism was actually born in Dublin from the pen of Richard Brinsley Sheridan who featured the word-bungling Mrs Malaprop in his play *The Rivals* in 1775. The present-day citizens of the capital carry on this proud tradition.**

Bertie Ahern (ET — the Ex-Taoiseach) was a great user of malapropisms, whether deliberately or accidentally, no one can tell. Here are a few:

> We will not upset the apple tart.
> There are kebabs out there plotting against me.
> There's a lot of smoke and dagger going on.

*

The late great Willie Bermingham of the Dublin Fire Brigade was a saintly man who did wonderful work to improve conditions for the poor, but he dropped malapropisms like hailstones:

> Willie once modestly refused recognition for his work saying, 'I don't expect a standing ovulation.'
> He offered help to the 'Sick and Indignant Roomkeeper's Association'.

*

Solomon had five hundred wives and seven hundred cucumbers.

*

A Dublin woman was introducing her daughter's boyfriend to the woman next door.

'This is my daughter's fiasco,' she announced.

*

A Dublin pub owner boasted that he had a muriel painted on one of his walls.

*

A bar stool politician commented on the number of Soviet agents who defecated to the west.

*

A Dublin woman took a holiday in the Sea Shells when an octobus attacked her in the water and wrapped his testicles around her.

*

A fellow in a pub was praising Yasser Marrowfat who did so much for the peas process.

*

Children in religious education classes in Dublin have claimed the first book in the Bible is the Book of Guinnesses.

*

Jesus was betrayed by Judas the Carrycot.

*

Mary was exposed to a man named Joseph.

*

God spoke to Moses from a burning bus.

*

The Wise Men brought gifts of gold, Frankenstein and myrrh.

*

Saint Paul was converted on the road to Domestos.

*

We believe in Heaven and Hell but not in puberty.

*

The Pope is inflammable.

*

A Dublin woman went to the doctor complaining of an attack of dire rear.

*

A Dublin chef went to Paris and was awarded the condom blue.

*

To prepare for the winter, a Moore Street trader bought some terminal underwear.

*

'That fellow is hung like a scallion,' said a Dublin girl of her boyfriend.

*

A Dublin woman nearly drowned in the sea but a lifeguard rescued her and gave her artificial insemination.

*

A Dubliner was proud that his son had a job at Trinity College. 'He's a lecherer,' he announced proudly.

*

A Dublin woman was not looking forward to the future. 'I'm afraid I will get Old Timer's disease,' she said.

*

A Dublin girl declared that she didn't use much makeup but liked to put a little massacre on her eyes.

*

A Dublin theatregoer went to see John Millicent Synge's *Ploughboy of the Western World*.

*

A Dublin woman claimed her twins were very alike — like two pees in a pot.

*

A Dubliner wasn't renowned for telling the truth — everything he said you had to take with a dose of salts.

*

She was taken short in O'Connell Street and had to use a public conveyance.

*

He used to love listening to the Queen's Speech on television at Christmas — the Vagina Monologue.

*

She has terrible trouble with her bladder — she's totally incompetent.

*

A certain actor I know is reputed to be a sexagenarian. At his age I think that is disgusting.

*

I think the law is too laxative on criminals.

# MOORE STREET

**Moore Street is Dublin's open fruit, vegetable and flower market just a stone's throw from the GPO. The many ladies who ply their wares there are known for their quick wit and that is no lie because I have heard them in action.**

A Moore street trader was having problems so she went to the doctor for an examination. 'Have you ever been incontinent?' he asked her.

'No doctor,' she told him, 'but I was in Liverpool for a weekend once.'

\*

Molly from Moore Street was a bit worried when the shops began to sell extremely realistic plastic flowers, so she shouted out to her mate: 'You should see the artificial flowers they are sellin' in Clerys. They are so lifelike they're unreal and they would deceive the bees.'

\*

The Moore Street traders once organised a tour of the cultural wonders of Italy. One of the first sights they encountered was the Leaning Tower of Pisa.

'Willya looka,' said one of the ladies, 'it's crooka.'

\*

A lady from Moore Street went to the doctor and found a queue of twenty people in front of her. Having waited for over an hour she stood up and announced, 'I think I'll go home and die a natural death.'

*

Biddy, a Moore Street trader, was over twenty stone, so the doctor put her on a strict diet. He arrived up at her house one day to find her tucking into a huge meal of steak and chips followed by Black Forest Gateau and ice cream.

'Biddy, Biddy,' he said to her, 'what about your diet?'

'Oh, I've had my diet, doctor,' she smiled, 'so now I'm having my dinner. Anyway, I'm not going to starve myself to death for the sake of living a few years longer.'

*

Two of the Moore Street stallholders fell out and were trading insults.

'Look at her,' shouted one, 'her teeth are like the ten commandments — all broken.'

*

A customer once asked a Moore Street lady how she was feeling.

'Oh, I feel like a little baby,' she replied.

'Full of life and looking forward to the future?' smiled the customer.

'No, no teeth, no hair, and I wet myself several times a day.'

*

The wit of Moore Street is not a new phenomenon — it goes back a long way. In the nineteenth century, a vicious-tongued harridan named Biddy Moriarty kept a huckster stall near the Four Courts, not a million miles from Moore Street. Nobody had ever got the better of Biddy in a slanging match, though many had tried. Daniel O'Connell, a Kerryman, later to be called the Liberator, was a young lawyer in Dublin, renowned for his eloquence at the bar, and his legal friends laid a large wager that he could not get the better of Biddy in a verbal contest. O'Connell had a cunning plan, reckoning rightly that Biddy would not be familiar with the higher mathematics. The dialogue went something like this:

*O'Connell:* What's the price of this walking-stick Mrs what's your name?

*Biddy:* Moriarty, sir, is my name, and a good one it is. And one-and-sixpence is the price of the stick. Truth, it's chape as dirt it is.

*O'Connell:* One and sixpence for a walking stick? You're no better than an impostor to ask eighteen pence for what cost you two pence.

*Biddy:* Two pence, your grandmother. Do you mane to say that it's chating the people I am? Impostor indeed.

*O'Connell:* Keep a civil tongue in your head you old diagonal.

*Biddy:* Stop your jaw, you pug-nosed badger, or by this and by that I'll make you go quicker nor you came.

*O'Connell:* Don't be in a passion, my old radius, anger will only wrinkle your beauty.

*Biddy:* You potato-faced, pippin-sneezer, when did a Madagascar monkey like you learn to hide your Kerry accent?

*O'Connell:* Easy now, you old whiskey-drinking parallelogram.

*Biddy:* What's that you call me? I'm none of your

parrybellygrums, you rascally gallows-bird; you cowardly, sneaking, plate-licking blaggard!

*O'Connell:* I suppose you'll deny you keep a hypotenuse in your house.

*Biddy:* It's a lie, you dirty robber, I never had such a thing in my house, you swindling thief.

*O'Connell:* Why sure all your neighbours know that you keep not only a hypotenuse, but you have two diameters locked up in your garret, and that you walk them every Sunday, you heartless old heptagon.

*Biddy:* May the devil fly away with you, you mitcher from Munster and make sauce of your rotten limbs, you mealy-mouthed tub of guts. Rinse your mouth in the Liffey, your mouth is filthier than your face, you dirty son of Beelzebub.

*O'Connell:* Rinse your own mouth, you wicked-minded old polygon.

Here Biddy was lost for words and O'Connell moved in for the kill: Look at her boys! There she stands, a convicted perpendicular in petticoats. There's contamination in her circumference and she trembles with guilt down to the extremities of her corollaries. Ah, I've found you out, you rectilinear antecedent, you equiangular old hag. The devil will fly away with you, you porter-swiping similitude of the bisection of a vertex.

Biddy was overwhelmed with the torrent of mathematical abuse, of which she understood not a word. She grabbed a saucepan and aimed it at O'Connell's head, but he beat a hasty retreat. All were agreed that he had won the wager.

*

One Moore Street trader was telling the stallholder next to her that her little boy was expelled from school because the lad next to him was smoking.

'That was a bit unfair, wasn't it?' said her mate.

'Maybe it was, but it was my lad who set him on fire.'

\*

'Have you any asparagus?' a Moore Street trader was asked by a customer.

'God help your sense love,' she replied. 'The only asparagus I have is in the veins in me legs.'

\*

A Moore Street lady was trading away merrily unaware that one of her voluminous breasts was hanging out. 'Mother of God,' said her neighbour, 'make yourself decent — one of your boobs is hanging out.'

'Oh my God,' said the lady, 'I must have left the baby on the bus.'

\*

'Bridie,' shouted one Moore Street trader, 'Diya think I look younger without me bra?'

'Well, it certainly takes the wrinkles out of yer face.'

\*

'I'm thinkin' of sending me son to university,' said one Moore Street trader to another, 'and makin' him into a doctor. Now whaddya think a that?'

'It'll never work luv — he'll never be able to write a prescription with a spray can.'

\*

A Dublin traffic warden showed up at a Moore Street stall, looked for a massive discount and when he didn't get it, went off without buying a single item. While he was still within earshot, the stallholder shouted to her neighbour: 'Bridie, why do you think those traffic wardens have a yellow stripe on their caps?'

'I dunno luv, why?'

'Maybe it's to stop people parking their cars on their heads.'

*

'What's the best thing for a black eye?' a lad asked a Moore Street trader.

'I find a punch in the face usually works,' she cackled.

*

'Have you got a match?' a cheeky young fella asked a lady of Moore Street.

'Yes son,' she told him, 'your face and my arse.'

*

'Look at him go,' a Moore Street trader shouted after a man passing by her stall. 'A typical Dubliner. Job in the Civil Service, house in Foxrock and a Cork accent.'

*

'Dublin is a wonderful city,' said one of the ladies in Moore Street. 'It's the only place in the world you can park your car, walk a few streets and find your tyres for sale.'

*

'I have a very sarcastic washing machine Bridie.'

'How is that Molly?'

'Well it keeps takin' the piss out of my knickers.'

# MISLEADING ADVICE FOR TOURISTS

**Dublin is a mecca for tourists from all over the world, but during the tourist season, Dubliners, out of pure devilment, have been known to give our visitors some unofficial advice, often with hilarious results. Here are a few examples that have spiced up many a visitor's experience of our capital city:**

On boarding the DART in Dublin, it is customary to shake hands with all the passengers.

*

Have you tried the famous echo in the reading-room of the National Library?

*

Irish Rail porters are traditionally known as gobshites. If you need help with your luggage, shout, 'I say, gobshite, can you give me a hand?' [Gobshite is Irish for 'a helpful servant'].

*

Not for nothing is Dublin known as the City of Singing Bus Drivers. Ask for your favourite song and they will be happy to oblige.

*

Loud and good-natured heckling from the public gallery of Dáil Éireann is a custom almost as old as the state itself.

*

Most restaurants provide a dish with small change for the convenience of tourists.

*

Wednesday is photograph day at the Four Courts. Pose with the colourfully-robed judges — it's a real treat for the kids.

*

You can still eat well in Dublin for €30 a day or less provided you confine yourself to certain restaurants. Membership of the circle is indicated by the five star symbol.

*

On first visiting a church it is customary to drink the entire contents of the holy water font.

*

Most small shops provide racks of postcards free for visitors. Take as many as you like.

*

Entry to Croke Park on All-Ireland final days is free to all overseas visitors, as long as they are wearing their chosen county colours.

*

All traditional musicians in pubs are strictly teetotal. Never insult these men by offering to buy them alcoholic drinks. Raspberry cordial is their preferred tipple.

*

Ladies of the night in Dublin traditionally dress as female

policemen. They will resist your approaches to add to the excitement of the occasion.

*

At the back of every church in Dublin, standing just outside the doorway on Sundays, you will find a group of men. These men are repentant sinners waiting to return to the faith, but they must be sponsored by someone from outside the parish. These men must be dragged up to the altar by the sponsor, saying aloud, 'I claim this man for Christ's sake.'

*

Why not buy a page from *The Book of Kells* in the library of Trinity College? The cost is just ten euro and a self-service system operates.

# A FINAL FLOURISH OF DUBLIN JOKES

A gorilla walks into a pub in Dublin and orders a pint of Guinness.

The terrified barman serves him and says, 'That will be ten euro, sir.'

As the gorilla drinks his pint, the barman tries to make conversation.

'Are you with the circus, sir? We don't get many gorillas in this bar.'

'At ten euro for a pint, I'm not surprised,' snaps the gorilla.

\*

A Dubliner is in hospital having had an operation to remove his appendix, when a priest friend comes in and tells him that his wife has just fallen down the stairs and broken her neck.

'Don't tell me any more,' says the Dub, 'or I'll burst me stitches.'

\*

Dublin gardaí made headlines all over the world in 2009, and even won an award in the coveted Ig Nobel competition. They issued over fifty driving tickets to a Polish gentleman named Mr Prawo Jazdy, until someone pointed out that 'prawo jazdy' is in fact Polish for 'driving licence'. So well done to the boys in blue!

*Extract from a tourist guide:* The smell of the Liffey is one of the finest sights in Dublin.

\*

The late Maureen Potter was one of Dublin's greatest comedians, and certainly the best loved. In partnership with Jimmy O'Dea, she set standards that will never be equalled. Her best creation was probably her feckless (and imaginary) son Christy whom she used as a mirror to reflect her opinions on Irish society, squeezing out a lot of laughs in the process. In one famous sketch, written as usual by Maureen's very talented husband Jack O'Leary, she buys Christy a pair of shoes in a shoe shop and he is given a gift of balloons. Immediately he is lifted up and floats away over Dublin — he's not floating down from a spaceship, he's floating up from a shoe shop. As he hovers over 'Cleary's', Maureen shouts, 'You'll never get in there with your Dublin accent', and as he approaches the Gresham Hotel she shouts, 'Keep away from there son we cannot afford it.' Finally he lands at the Rotunda Maternity Hospital prompting the headline: 'Ten Stone Boy Delivered in the Rotunda! Mother and Child Doing Well!'

\*

Maureen once related that she heard the following conversation between two little girls in the Gaiety Theatre:

    'Have you school tomorrow?'

    'Yeah.'

    'Wha have yiz got?'

    'English. What have you got?'

    'Ele-KEW-tion! I HAY-RITT.'

\*

I once had the privilege of seeing the great Maureen Potter on the stage of the Gaiety Theatre in Dublin. Danny Cummins played her husband and Chris Curran her oversized son. The couple were attempting to explain, very belatedly, the facts of life to their forty-year-old son, dressed in short trousers:

'All those people walking round the streets of Dublin,' she said to him, 'have you ever wondered where they came from?'

'Sure I know very well,' he told them.

'Where did they come from?' they asked in amazement.

'Up from Cork,' he smiled in triumph.

\*

A Dubliner had a severe heart condition so his doctor advised him to avoid excitement. So now he watches only League of Ireland football matches.

\*

A startling statistic — more time is lost to industry in Dublin by workers visiting the toilet than through strikes.

\*

A Dublin woman and her kid were in McDonald's.

'Diya want a coke?' she asked him.

'Ha?' he replied.

'Look, I've told you a hundred times, it's not "ha?" it's "wha?"'

\*

Brendan Grace is one of Dublin's best-loved comedians and has been for years. His best-known creation is Bottler, the quintessential Dublin delinquent and my favourite sketch is where Bottler goes to confession — the priest is behind a cast iron grill complete with protective Alsatian. Bottler tells his sins and for his penance the priest tells him to say a Hail Mary.

'I don't know that prayer, father,' says Bottler.

'Well say an Our Father, then.'

'I don't know that prayer either, father.'

'Well what prayer do you know?'

'The Angelus, father.'

'Well say that then.'

Bottler goes, 'Boing, boing, boing.'

*

The irreverent undergraduates of Trinity College, Dublin University, have been known to refer to the *Book of Kells*, that unique and priceless treasure housed in the college library and one of Ireland's biggest tourist attractions, as 'Kelly's Book'.

*

This Dubliner bought a carpet 'in mint condition' for €10 at a sale. Right enough, when he brought it home he found there was a hole in the middle.

*

This Dubliner went to the doctor and when he took off his hat, the doctor was amazed to see a strawberry growing out of his head.

'Can you help me?' asked the patient.

'Yes,' said the doctor, 'I can give you some cream to put on that.'

*

A Dublin woman reported to the police that her husband was missing.

After a few weeks, the police called round to her house and told her that they had found his body floating in the Liffey.

'Oh that couldn't be him,' she told them, 'my husband couldn't swim.'

*

The great Dublin comedian Jimmy O'Dea once defined Dublin snobbery as 'all fur coat and no knickers'.

*

One of Dublin's best-known boozers was feeling a bit under the weather so he went to the doctor. The doctor sent him for tests and when the results of the tests came back the diagnosis was — too much blood in his alcohol stream.

*

Two Dubliners decided to meet in Rome for a European Cup match.

'Where will we get together?' asked one.

'How about the Vatican?'

'Right,' says the other, 'in the bar or the lounge?'

*

Two nuns were collecting in a pub on a Saturday night when they were confronted by a well-oiled Dubliner.

'Who are youse?' he enquired suspiciously.

'We're the Sisters of John the Baptist,' answered one of the nuns meekly.

'Get along outta that,' said the well-oiled gentleman, 'yez is not foolin' me — John the Baptist is dead for over 2,000 years.'

*

This guy was having a drink in a bar on Dublin's southside (well it makes a change, doesn't it?).

A fellow said to him, 'Would you like to buy an expensive gold watch for a tenner?'

'OK,' said the guy, 'show it to me.'

'Ssh,' said the fellow, 'the bloke next to you is wearing it.'

*

A Dubliner came home one night to find his wife lying in bed dressed in a flimsy outfit.

'Tie me up,' she said passionately, 'and you can do anything you like.'

So he tied her up and went down to the pub.

*

A Dubliner had a fierce shake in his hands, desperate it was, so he decided to go to the doctor.

'Do you drink a lot?' the doctor asked him.

'What would be a lot?' the Dub asked.

'Well,' said the doctor, 'say five pints a night.'

'Jaysus doc, I spill more than that.'

*

A fellow up from the country is driving through Dublin when he gets a puncture. So he jacks the car up and is changing the flat tyre when he notices a little Dubliner opening his boot with a lever.

'Hey you,' he shouts, 'bugger off, this is my car.'

'Don't be greedy,' says the Dub, 'you do the front half and I'll do the back.'

*

What do you call a thirty-stone Dublin stripper?

Unemployed!

*

Two Dublin trade unionists were discussing the coming of spring.

'I see the snowdrops and the daffodils are out,' says one.

'How will that affect us?' asked the other.

*

How do you recognise a passionate Dubliner?

He puts out his fag and swallows his phlegm before he kisses a girl.

*

The average Dublin man's attitude to marriage is — why acquire a whole cow when you can drink as much milk as you want cheap? But the average Dublin woman retaliates by saying — why do you need to tolerate a whole pig when all you want is a sausage.

*

What is black and white and tells the archbishop of Dublin to get lost?

A nun who has just won the Lotto.

*

Never ask a man where he's from.

If he's from Dublin, he'll tell you soon enough.

And if he's not, why embarrass him?

*

This time it is the grandmothers of the two auld wans, appearing for the very last time in this book.

Two really auld wans were riding in an omnibus in

1917. 'How is your son getting on in the army?' asked the first.

'Oh, he was shot in the Dardanelles,' said the second.

'That's terrible,' said the first, 'I believe that's a very painful spot.'

\*

A Dublin economist picked up a taxi at Dublin airport and was being driven to his office at the International Financial Services Centre. Disgusted at his tip, the taxi driver nodded in the direction of Ireland's premier development and said, 'Canary Dwarf, wha?'

\*

In Dublin, a fellow with a strong libido is often described as being, 'a martyr for de quare ting'.

\*

A certain order of priests in Dublin is often referred to as 'the passionate fathers with the loose habits'.

\*

For some reason or other, Dubliners have a great turn of phrase when it comes to describing the extremes of hunger pangs. Here a few of their poetic outpourings:

> I'm that hungry I could eat a nun's arse through the convent railings.
> I'm that hungry I could eat the balls off a low-flying duck.
> I'm that hungry I could eat a dead Christian Brother.
> Me stomach thinks me throat's been cut.
> I could eat a farmer's arse through a blackthorn bush.
> I could eat a bull between two bread vans.

I'm that hungry I could eat the scabby leg off a septic
leper.

I'm so hungry I could eat the back door if it was
buttered.

I told the barman to stop scratchin' his arse and make
me a sandwich.

*

This fellow from Tallaght went into a chemist's shop and
asked if he could buy some arsenic. 'What do you want
it for?' he was asked.

'To poison the wife,' said the fellow.

'I'm sorry,' said the chemist, 'I can't sell you that.'

The fellow then produced a picture of his wife.

'I'm sorry sir,' said the chemist, producing a big bottle
of arsenic, 'I didn't realise you had a prescription.'

*

The great Samuel Johnson in 1779 paid Dublin the
following backhanded compliment: 'Dublin, though a
place much worse than London, is not so bad as Iceland.'

*

They say you can always tell a Dubliner — but you can't
tell him much.

*

One Dubliner was boasting to another in a bar about what
a fine child he was. 'When I was born,' he told him, 'I
weighed twelve pounds, but the next day I weighed only
nine pounds.'

'How the hell did that come about?' asked his mate.

'I was circumcised,' said the Dubliner.

*

There was this man living in the high rise apartments in Dublin's Ballymun and fierce holy he was altogether, and he was known locally as Blessed Barnabas of Ballymun. All the residents felt that he should be declared a saint so they chartered a plane to Rome to petition the Pope for him to be canonised as Saint Barnabas of Ballymun.

The Holy Father graciously granted the deputation an audience and listened to their petition. 'Blessed Barnabas was a really holy man,' said the chairwoman. 'He attended Mass every morning of his life, did an awful lot of good in the community and gave away all his possessions to the poor.'

'Very good,' said the Pope, 'but before he can be elevated to sainthood, there must be evidence of a miracle. Have there been any miracles due to the intercession of Blessed Barnabas?'

'Yes, Your Holiness,' said the chairwoman, and a little Dublin lad stepped forward to speak.

'Well, one night,' said the chiseller, 'Blessed Barnabas went into a pub where there were lots of bad men smokin' cigarettes and drinkin' pints of porter. Blessed Barnabas said loudly, "This is a nest of vipers and a den of iniquity" an' he went over and pulled the cigarettes from their mouths and plunged them into their pints of porter.'

'Very good,' said the Pope, 'but where is the miracle?'

'Jaysus,' said the chiseller, 'it's a miracle he wasn't killed!'